Boys and Girls at Play

NORMAN ROCKWELL'S

Boys and

George Mendoza

Girls at Play

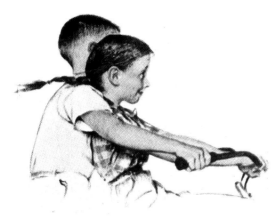

Harry N. Abrams, Inc., Publishers, New York

For Ashley and Ryan with love ...

Library of Congress Cataloging in Publication Data

Mendoza, George.
    Norman Rockwell's boys and girls at play.

    SUMMARY: Norman Rockwell's illustrations of children
at play accompany a poem.

    [1. Friendship—Poetry] I. Rockwell, Norman,
1894- II. Title.
PZ8.3.M55164No 811'.5'4 76-18674
ISBN 0-8109-1352-6

Library of Congress Catalogue Card No: 76-18674
Copyright © 1976 by Harry N. Abrams, Incorporated, New York

And where do you take me?

Across the mountains

as tall as my mind ...?

Skipping seas that sail up

my dreams ...?

Where do you take me?

Do you know the place

I seek called forever,

the Land of Enchantment.

O let me hear

dreams that rainbow the sky,

songs that lift the hills,

and tomorrows that echo

boys and girls at play ...

   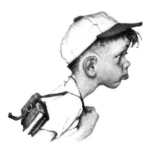

And I'll follow you

waking meadow and wood

where clouds are fishing

upon the deep pools clear ...

I'll sail with you

when you say ready, mate,

there's gold in the pocket

of every tree …

I'll run away with you,

catch the long night train with you.

And we'll whistle down the rails

and dusty roads …

I'll pretend you are the princess

and I your prince,

"Will you marry me, my darling?

I'll be lonely, so sad,

if you say, no, you won't ..."

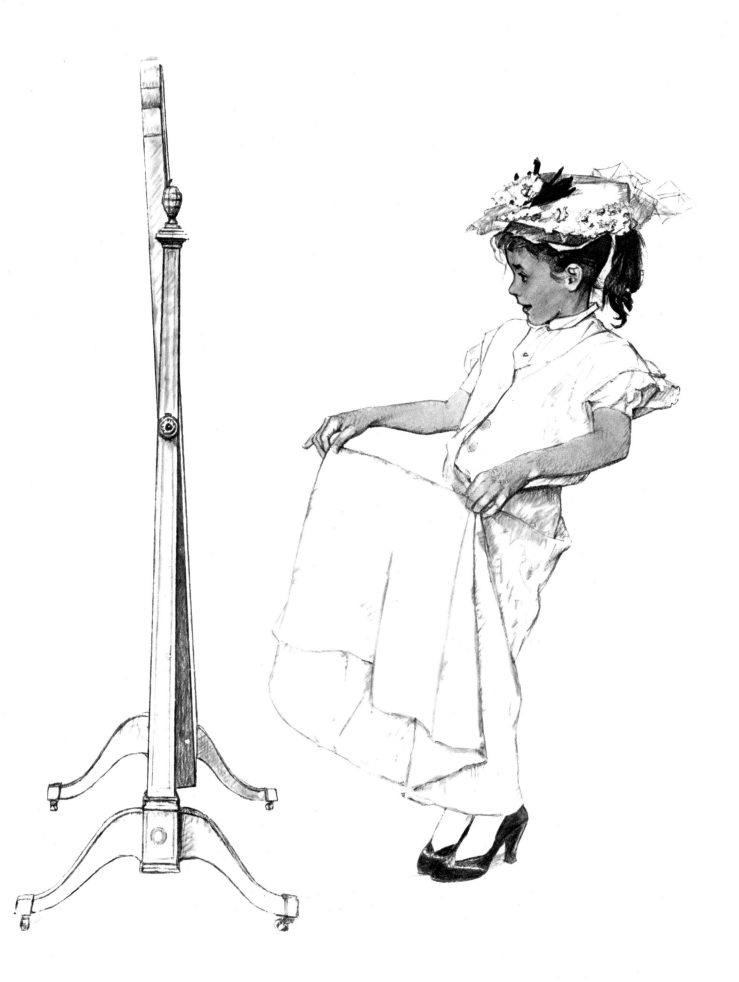

I'll race with you,

spin time with you.

Watch out old world,

we're coming through …

16

I'll take a chance with you ...

I'll dance with you …

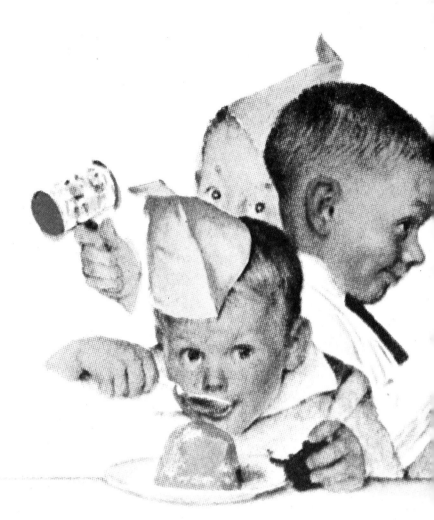

I'll blow away the years with you ...

As long as dreams of play

stay upside down in your head …

I'll be there to cheer for you ...

I'll be a fool with you ...

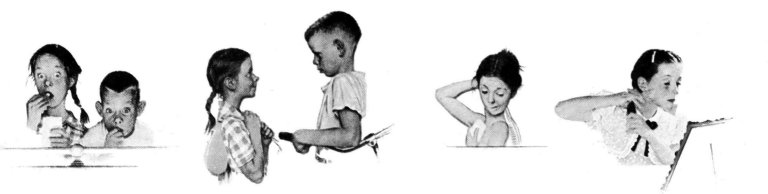

HIGH DIVE
20 FEET

Norman Rockwell

I'll be as daring

as an eagle with you …

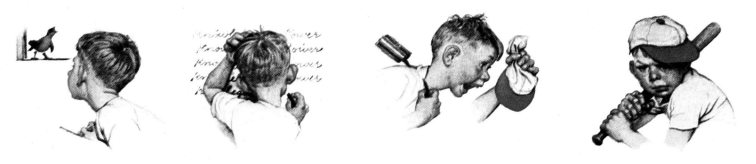

I'll bet with you

even when I know

you've won ...

I'll curl up alone with you

against the nest of a hill

where flutes of grass are playing …

I'll jump with joy with you ...

I'll feel with you,

the beginnings of all our feelings ...

I'll sniff golden leaves

of falling poems with you …

I'll find the way with you ...

I'll become a man with you …

I'll see the world with you ...

I'll turn the seasons with you ...

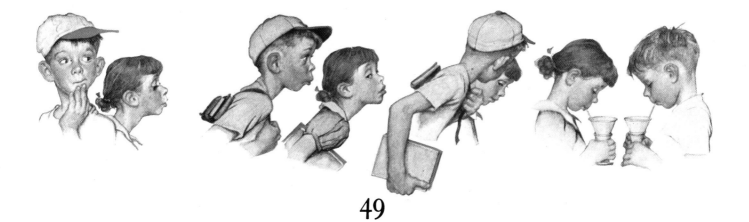

I'll believe with you

a wish can stop the world ...

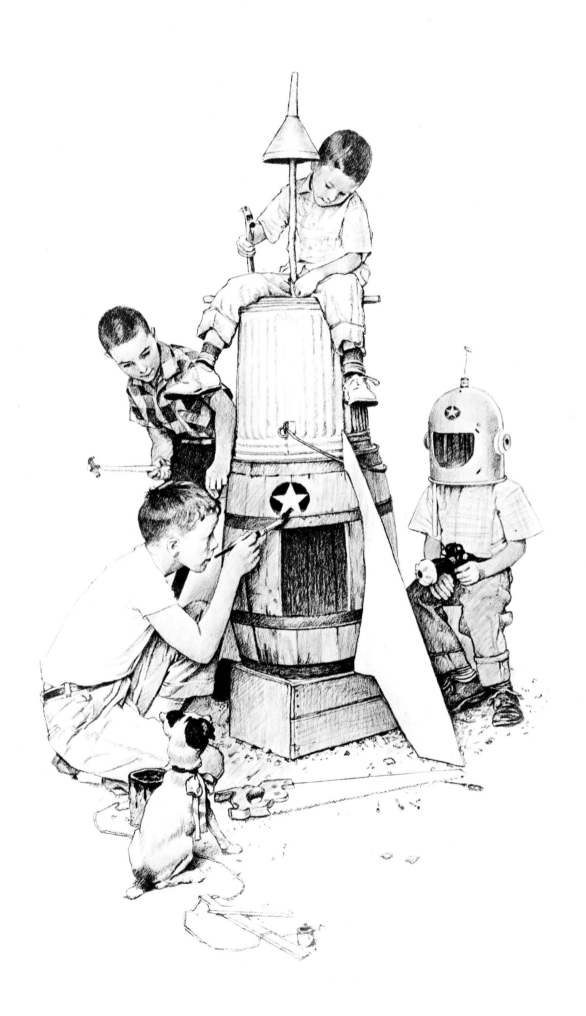

I'll go up with you ...

. . . and down with you . . .

I'll grow up with you ...

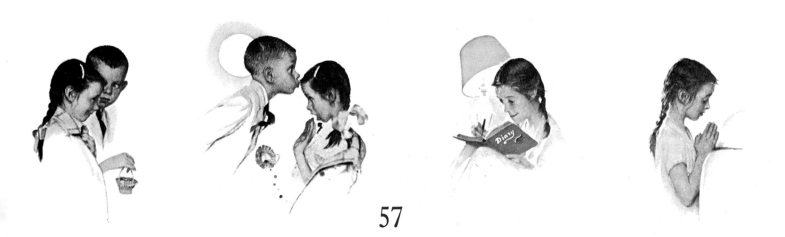

And we'll play, boys and girls,

till we're children all over again ...

LIST OF ILLUSTRATIONS